MW00625020

Three words: Introspective, Foundational, and Timeless. I have had the distinct pleasure of working with Andrea Chilcote over the years as an executive coach for me personally, an executive coach for executives I have led, and as facilitator for executive team transformations. *What Leaders Need Now* and the principles Andrea pronounces in this book not only call out what is needed now but it is really what leaders needed at their core way of being all along: "compassion, courage and humility." The pandemic certainly called these imperative leadership qualities to the forefront, and as Andrea points out, leaders with the grit and self-discipline to grow and develop in these areas are the models of the past and our future. The book reminds me as a leader to celebrate the good and bad from the seasons of life and use each experience to enrich the lives of others. It also reinforces leadership and life is a series of reflection and reinvention points we must have to serve others to the best of our ability.

—*Shawn C. Duncan*
Vice President Field Operations
at Cox Communications

What Leaders Need Now inspires one to take action, regardless of one's function, title, or level in an organizational chart. This readable and enjoyable book presents a beautiful medley of data, research, poetry, and Andrea's personal experience and her observations and anecdotes gleaned from years of working with leaders and individuals being coached for leadership positions. Whether you are the head of a large organization, a department leader, supervisor of a small team or even a solopreneur, this book offers a powerful framework and guidance for being the kind of leader the world needs now. Take your time reading it: savor her words and insight, reflect with the prompts provided in each chapter, and know that Andrea Chilcote, an intuitive, thoughtful, and skilled leadership coach, will never steer you wrong.

—Stefanie Borsari
Principal and Founder
Stefanie Borsari Consulting LLC

Whether in the private, public, or nonprofit sectors, executives and managers are at no loss for a bevy of books and resources telling them how to be better leaders. But what the market and thus everyday leaders and aspiring leaders lack is a resource that is easily accessible, digestible and provides the concepts and tools to transform the personal and professional to benefit any organization. In *What Leaders Need Now*, Andrea gives us the gift of brevity, compelling examples and synthesizes various leadership theories and current data to effectively show us why we should and how we can all lead with compassion, courage and humility and empower others to do the same. I have personally witnessed her inspire others as a leader and she is the embodiment of the qualities she deftly offers up the reader as critical tools required now as much as ever in current culture. I am confident this book will help me in my current professional role and look forward to sharing it with colleagues and other change-makers.

—Kellye Pinkleton
Director, Public Policy, Companion Animals
The Humane Society of the United States

Much has been said, written and lamented about leadership; finally, here is a guide for what the world needs now, as beautifully articulated by Andrea Chilcote. Indeed the world has changed and so has humanity . . . what was needed decades ago is very different as our world has reshaped. Andrea's exploration of the qualities of compassion, courage, and humility are paramount to creating a better world within families and organizations, and everyone will benefit from the pleasure of this read. This is a refreshing, wise and timely guide to help all of us make our world a better and more meaningful place.

—Joette Schmidt

Andrea has insights that will connect you with your own inner strengths and will guide you to a place where you can engage your courage as a leader and person. She points toward universal leadership traits that will inspire a more human workplace where leaders and team members will thrive. Beyond SMART goals and annual plans, this book offers a more inspiring and compelling vision for leaders to embrace.

—Jack Skalican, Ed.D.
Leadership scholar

The author masterfully distills her extensive leadership experience, research, and observations into three inner qualities: compassion, courage, and humility. Through personal stories, thoughtful questions, and gentle guidance, she demonstrates their relevance and critical importance in today's widely varied work environments. Leaders, from beginner to expert, will find this book packed with deep wisdom and distinctive practices to positively influence the way they lead and impact results.

—Janice Jernigan,
author of *Opening Up to Grief*

When I met Andrea Chilcote over two decades ago, I admired her commitment to distinct, short, and applicable learning bites. Her laser-focus on a skill that leaders can implement immediately, measure the impact, and accept the outcome as a gift shows up again in *What Leaders Need Now*. If you are ready to embrace the adventure of growing with ease, simplicity, and wisdom, you need to read this book NOW.

—Betsy Corley Pickren
Chief Leadership Coach and Advisor
WoodFire Leadership

WHAT LEADERS NEED NOW

Inner Qualities and Essential Practices

Andrea Chilcote

ISBN: 978-0-9882927-4-1 (softcover)
ISBN: 978-0-9882927-5-8 (e-book)

Published by Morningstar Ventures Inc.
www.morningstarventures.com

This book is dedicated with love and gratitude to Laura Roccaforte and Randy Hain, without whose fierce acknowledgment this book would be only an idea in my mind rather than a tangible call to transformation.

CONTENTS

INTRODUCTION

What Leaders Need Now

In early March of 2020, before the emerging pandemic had revealed itself to be the protracted, tragic reality that would change our lives in profound ways, my colleagues and I set out to study what leaders needed most amidst the uncertainty of being thrust into a virtual world in which no operating manual existed. In the past two and a half years, I have learned more about what leaders *really* need than I have working as an executive coach for the past twenty. Leaders have needed these things all along, of course, and we'll surely need them in the future. Yet, the conditions of the past thirty-six months have conspired to highlight what we need when we are at our most vulnerable and have the most at stake. To say "leadership has never been more important" may sound cliché, yet so it is.

What leaders need are the same things followers

need *from* leaders: to recognize the human needs we all share in this time of great change. Consider that statement as you read this list:

- compassion
- courage
- humility

These are *inner* qualities—not core motivators that, while intrinsic themselves, are dependent on one's environment. If, as I do, you subscribe to Daniel Pink's theory that we are motivated by three elements—autonomy, purpose, and mastery—you might conclude that the qualities that leaders need now *enable* these motivators.

The three qualities—compassion, courage, and humility—are not skills to be learned or tools to be utilized. They are not personality traits or talents that a privileged few are born with. They are internal capabilities that can be grown, honed, and nurtured if one has the will to do so.

You might know a leader who possesses all three of these qualities. It's likely this did not come about by chance. Leaders who have reached a place in which these qualities are part of their essential nature have traveled a long and possibly difficult road of self-development. Those who demonstrate an ease with compassion, courage, and humility seem to derive their ability to do so from three essential practices:

- development
- reflection
- acknowledgment

In the following pages, we'll define the three inner qualities of compassion, courage, and humility, and look at how the three essential practices lead to their development in a leader. In subsequent chapters, we explore the qualities in depth, the ways in which they impact and influence one another, and practical ways to utilize development, reflection, and acknowledgment to begin to embody the leader at the heart of your being.

ONE

Inner Qualities and Essential Practices: An Overview

In this chapter we provide an overview of the three inner qualities leaders need more than ever in today's climate, and the essential practices to bring them to life.

Compassion

> *Times have changed, and people*
> *need people who actually care.*
>
> —A FRUSTRATED LEADER

One of my clients, Rebecca, was preparing to lead a very difficult organizational change as a new executive leader. Since it was during the pandemic, everything would need to be accomplished virtually. This was uncharted territory for her, and she was feeling out of her element. I suggested to Rebecca that her great capacity for empathy was her superpower. This woman is a model for compassionate leadership. She is also steadfast and decisive, unafraid to set high standards, and delivers appropriate and timely feedback. She does all of this in a way that is uplifting, supportive, and gracious. She connects with people on a *human* level, and as a result, they feel seen, heard, and understood. Her authentic empathy paved the way for her to perform at her best.

The word *compassion* stems from the Latin *compati*, meaning "to suffer with." According to the Dalai Lama, it is "an openness to the suffering of others with a commitment to relieve it."

Compassion is empathy with a desire to be in action. James R. Doty, MD, Stanford University professor and the director of The Center for Compassion and Altruism Research and Education at Stanford's School of Medicine (CCARE), explains this clearly and simply. He says that while our experiences can lead to fear, anxiety, stress, and an uncertain future, we always have a choice. "We can choose fear or love, and that choice requires compassion: compassion for ourselves and for others."[1]

Over the past two years, I've watched many compassionate leaders care for others, some heroically. These leaders also needed to care for themselves, and those who did not often found themselves in crisis.

What we as leaders need really has not changed. But we are no longer able to avoid the consequences of not caring for ourselves as well, something many of us have been avoiding for too long.

What is self-compassion? I don't always use that term in discussions with clients, but the impact of its absence arises frequently in our conversations. Dr. Kristin Neff contrasts the components of self-compassion's positive and negative constructs:[2]

- being kind and understanding toward oneself rather than being self-critical
- seeing one's fallibility as being part of the larger human condition rather than as isolating
- holding one's painful thoughts and feelings in mindful awareness rather than avoiding or overidentifying with them

Courage

"Get a good job," a parent says, meaning "Get a safe job." As if, over the years, they have learned the wicked, veering manner of the winds that blow through life in their unmerciful ways; but also they are passing on, parent to child, a fear bred into our human bones of that dark outer wind's howling, pushing presence.

—DAVID WHYTE[3]

I'm not sure we will ever witness acts of courage as profound as those of seemingly ordinary people—hospital leaders as well as frontline clinical workers—just doing their jobs over the past three years. There is no greater example of courage than those who risk their lives for others, whether in healthcare or another line of service. During the COVID-19 pandemic, courage was demonstrated in so many ways, in organizations both "essential" and "nonessential."

I recall an account of a vulnerable conversation between a mid-level leader and a CEO about her family that might never have occurred in ordinary circumstances. In that moment, they were simply two parents with a common concern for their children. But the conversation led, in part, to a courageous organizational decision on the part of that CEO. He realized in that moment how much power he had to influence thousands of families in a positive way, though not without risk of controversy. Countless other courageous micro-decisions were made at this time, simply because someone was brave enough to step up, take a stand, and act.

What do leaders need now? I posit that we need courage, and a lot of it. The extraordinary engagement that occurred when leaders modeled courage during the COVID crisis led my colleagues and me to wonder, "Will this way of being remain after the crisis has passed?"

It's too soon to fully answer that question. The absence of courage is still on display. Just yesterday a client told me his mentor gave him this advice: "Always agree with the executive's ideas in the meeting, then do what you need to do afterward." This is not an isolated incident; it happens in conference rooms everywhere. But this is not leadership, and it's the opposite of courage.

According to a 2012 Catalyst survey, "showing integrity" and "speaking truth to power'" were named as components of gravitas, one of the core characteristics of executive presence (EP). Sixty-four percent say it contributes to a woman's EP, 63 percent say it contributes to a man's, and this component beat emotional intelligence, reputation, and vision.[4] It takes courage to speak up to power.

Humility

If you google "humility" as a leadership trait or quality, you will see troves of articles touting practices by which leaders can employ skills such as asking questions, listening and promoting others, building emotional intelligence, and fostering collaboration. They sound a lot like components of Robert Greenleaf's classic Servant Leadership concept of "serve first." He says:

[Servant Leadership] manifests itself in the care taken by the servant-first to make sure that other people's highest priority needs are being served. The best test, and difficult to administer, is: Do those served grow as persons? Do they, while being served, become healthier, wiser, freer, more autonomous, more likely themselves to become servants?[5]

In my experience, servant leadership is dependent on leaders' innate ability to subordinate their ego needs to the needs of the constituents. This requires humility, an "other-centeredness," in a leader. It does not mean you have a low opinion of yourself, but it does require acknowledging your shortcomings—your "humiliations," if you will.

It still surprises me when leaders squirm at the idea of showing their weaknesses or admitting to mistakes. And yet research shows this kind of vulnerability and honesty creates trust in one's followers. Michelle Reina of Reina Trust Building puts twenty-five years of trust-focused research and experience behind this statement: "When you admit you've made a mistake, you don't erode trust in your leadership, you strengthen it." She says taking responsibility for mistakes makes us fallible humans (and thus relatable), conveys integrity, and creates the sense that it's safe for us and others to do the same.

Humble leaders seem to have a good gauge of appropriate transparency, perhaps because they don't have ego-driven agendas. One of my executive clients is a good example of this kind of humility. If you knew Ben, you would describe him as confident, engaging, perhaps even charismatic. If you knew him well, you would know how much he cares about his team, his organization, his community, and his family. Currently, Ben is going through a challenging period in which his own future role is uncertain. While I know how much this weighs on him personally, he is choosing to focus on the needs of his team. And he seems to know exactly how to be humanly vulnerable with his team in a way that does not fuel their fears and allows them to recognize and rely on their personal empowerment.

As leaders, compassion, courage, and humility are not qualities that we are born having a special knack for. And they are not traits we can learn simply from attending a leadership course. The essential practices that follow are necessary to unearth the potential in all of us for compassion, courage, and humility.

Our essence has been conditioned and shaped through our early history and the habits we've built in work and life over many, many years. The essential practices of development, reflection, and acknowledgment allow us to begin to examine our beliefs, behaviors, and values and commit to being leaders who are most needed now in the workplace and in our communities.

The Three Essential Practices

Development

> *True self is true friend. One ignores or rejects such friendship only at one's peril.*
>
> —PARKER PALMER[6]

By *development*, I don't mean training classes, SMART goals, or annual development plans. Development, as a practice for leaders, is the process by which we cast a vision for the future that is congruent with our true nature and desires, and in doing so, identify and work through the personal stops along the way. Part of the development journey is to make conscious the unconscious patterns and habits that have formed over a lifetime, to examine and assess their effectiveness in one's current life. It's the mechanism through which transformation occurs.

Richard Rohr, Franciscan priest and founder of the Center for Action and Contemplation in Albuquerque, New Mexico, says:

Any attempt to engineer or plan your own enlightenment will be doomed to failure because it will be ego-driven. You will only see what you've already decided to look for, and you cannot see what you are not ready or have been told to look for.[7]

I can attest that this sage wisdom plays out in my own life and in my work as a coach. I don't know anyone who has ever changed because someone told them to. The most painful work for a coach is to watch or assist someone who is making change under duress: the pressure of a boss or an undesired shift in strategic direction. This kind of change is temporary and disingenuous. So how do we honor Father Rohr's advice? Are we to wait around until a life crisis hits?

Reflection

Leadership is a human endeavor, yet the pace is inhuman. The big question is, how do you deal with it?
—KEVIN CASHMAN, GLOBAL COLEADER OF CEO AND EXECUTIVE LEADER DEVELOPMENT AT KORN FERRY

One of the challenges many of us would admit to is not taking enough time for reflection. As far as my qualifications to write on this topic go, I'm probably about five minutes ahead of many of the readers and perhaps a bit behind others, like my friend and colleague Randy Hain. His latest book, *Upon Reflection,* is designed as a guide for intentional reflection on key leadership practices. He says:

> The greatest contributor to my personal growth has been gazing into the past with a desire to learn and apply the lessons I glean versus peering into the future and seeking what's next.[8]

When soliciting feedback, executive coaches often hear the term *executive presence* on the "needs to improve" list. We follow that with a question to specify exactly what is meant by the phrase, as executive presence (EP) can mean anything from the quality of one's PowerPoint presentations to one's integrity. One time, my client described one of his leaders who lacked EP this way: "He's overscheduled. He rushes from one meeting to the next and doesn't take a breath in between. That's not executive behavior. I can't trust that he is making sound decisions for our organization if he doesn't make time to reflect."

I think we are sometimes afraid of being silent with ourselves. Yet without healthy reflection, our minds can turn to rumination, the unhealthy process of turning thoughts repeatedly, churning regretful thoughts about the past and anxious thoughts about the future. And unfortunately, this rumination occurs for many of us in the middle of the night.

Reflection is part of the answer to the dilemma Richard Rohr posed. If we pause, we will hear the beckoning. We will see anew. We might be presented with new choices.

Acknowledgment

Acknowledgment: acceptance of
the truth or existence of something.
—OXFORD ENGLISH DICTIONARY

Acknowledgment is a practice that accomplishes so many important purposes. It can indicate that you understand or accept something. It can be an admission of a mistake. Acknowledgment can be a show of gratitude or recognition. Acknowledgment in communication can validate another's feelings, as well as recognize their positive intent or point of view. Throughout my twenty years as a coach, these very common themes I see are:

- Leaders who struggle to positively acknowledge team members
- Leaders who struggle to accept positive acknowledgment

- Leaders who struggle because they themselves are not seen or heard (acknowledged)
- Leaders who cannot acknowledge critical feedback

Practicing self-acknowledgment builds self-compassion. While compassion for others as well as oneself has been studied significantly, only recently has research emerged presenting a significant correlation between the two. In this book, I treat them as equally important subsets of one quality without implying that building one impacts the other. Thus, I address self-acknowledgment and acknowledgment of others as distinct practices where appropriate.

Having moved to California two years ago, I recently gathered the courage to try surfing. To my dismay, I never was able to rise onto the board on the unstable water. I admittedly had fun bodyboarding, and I loved being in the ocean, yet it was an experience that left me feeling less than kind toward my sixty-year-old, imperfect body.

I recounted the experience to my wise osteopathic physician, Dr. Kate Perry. I asked her what she thought of the idea of me building the strength I needed to surf. It seems silly as I write this, but I brought her a video of the twenty-year-old friend who accompanied me on the adventure. She said, "Well, you could do that. Or you could accept the wonder that is you."

The wonder that is you. Try that on for a dose of self-acknowledgment when your inner critic admonishes you for some imperfection you hold as (falsely?) true.

Time to Reflect

At the end of each chapter, I will provide three reflection questions. These questions are intended to help you more consciously consider your own leadership development journey.

1. What did you agree with strongly, and/or disagree with strongly?
2. What evoked an emotional response, and possibly even suggested an area of personal vulnerability?
3. What one thing calls you to act, from a development perspective?

TWO

The Case for Compassion

Over the last three years, my team has closely followed data surrounding the factors that lead to burnout, a condition characterized by emotional exhaustion, a cynical attitude, and dissatisfaction with one's own performance. The amount of personal and workplace stress has increased at alarming rates, due to many factors, including rapidly shifting and competing priorities in an environment where the ways in which we communicate and connect have fundamentally changed.

In September of 2022, the Wiley Organization asked 5,014 professionals, individual contributors, and C-suite executives about burnout. Ninety-seven percent reported experiencing some level of work-related stress and a shocking 86 percent reported feelings of burnout.[9]

Something has to give.

I've been disturbed by the term *quiet quitting* since its inception. Quiet quitting, of course, is the phenomenon describing doing "just enough" to complete one's job but not going above and beyond. What I'm about to say may be heresy, but here goes: When did we begin expecting more than is expected?

I'm currently helping a client navigate several new job opportunities. Elyn, a senior vice president, tells me she is committed to setting boundaries on her time and wants to establish that up front before accepting a role. Good plan, I tell her. It's fascinating for me to observe her articulate her so-called boundaries, walk them back, then hear herself do so. It goes something like this: "I want to have my weekends to myself. I'll work long hours during the week, but I need to recharge on the weekend. I mean, I'll work on the weekend, but it must be on my schedule, not someone else's expectation that I will be available at a given time. Six days—yes, I'll work six days if I have one off." I asked her if it was unrealistic, in her experience, that a mid-level or senior leader could work only five days a week. She said, "Yes, unrealistic." Wow.

In a Wiley Workplace Research Article, the Wiley Organization takes an important stand when they say: "In fact, Quiet Quitting is a bit of a misnomer, as individuals are not quitting their jobs, but instead are embracing more healthy boundaries around their work lives as a result of burnout."[10]

Organizations that see people as only resources to be utilized in the service of producing or providing for the organization are losing employees. That is a fact. Employees at all levels are experiencing stress and burnout, and as leaders, many of us are not paying attention to what's going on around us.

I'm working with a leader, Darren, who just received some necessary and difficult-to-hear feedback. Members of his team told him that he doesn't listen when they tell him that timelines are simply unrealistic or that so-called priorities are too numerous to be considered such. They wondered where the empathetic leader they had once known had gone. The feedback was sobering, and he listened. After consideration, he concluded that he had allowed himself to get too busy to pay attention, too tough to listen, too driven to step back and reflect. Darren is not a leader who doesn't care about people, though his conduct would suggest that. It took a jolt to awaken him to the realization that people were hurting because of his behavior. Almost immediately, he began making changes. The empathetic leader, the one able to step into the shoes of another and view the world from their eyes, is returning, though not without a lot of hard work.

Darren couldn't do this on his own. It took a crisis of

sorts, an intervention by those who knew of his potential for compassionate leadership, to hold up a feedback mirror. And it took his commitment to development to be willing to look in that mirror.

Reading this, some of you might feel disdain for this leader, especially if you've been the recipient of this kind of behavior or have watched someone make disingenuous attempts to reengage a beleaguered team. If so, for a moment consider this man as not just an individual but as an archetype. This archetype is the leader we create when we impose years of fear-based, command-and-control conditioning on employees advancing through their careers.

We know well the impact of emotional trauma on children in their formative years, but what of the trauma that is inflicted in toxic corporate cultures? Years of conditioning can form patterns of behavior, the cause of which remains unconscious until brought into awareness. This can be carried from role to role, company to company, as it is not changed simply by a refresh in one's external environment. This is one reason why it's so hard for a new leader to "change the culture" when there has been a history of fear, deference to authority, bullying, or other such markers of an unhealthy environment.

In the case of my client, we could consider offering the services of a coach and putting in place a process of feedback, however painful, as an act of compassion. Someone—in this case, Darren's immediate leader—first considered positive intent on his part: "What is the possible positive reason he might be doing what he is doing?" Of course, asking this question requires extending empathy, and empathy—along with its active cousin compassion—is the first step to unpacking the armor to reveal the leader within.

Compassion: Empathy in Action

In the previous chapter, I suggest that compassion is "empathy with a desire to be in action." Let's first take a look at what empathy is—and is not.

What Empathy Is Not

Empathy is not "what I would think or feel if I were you." If I had someone else's situation, I would naturally respond in different ways because my experiences, personality, likes and dislikes, and values are different.

Let's look at a simple example. I have a friend who does not like garlic, not at all. I happen to love it. So let's suppose she receives a garlic gift basket on her birthday from Gilroy, California, the garlic capital of the world. I would, if *I* were her, feel thrilled. But because I am not the one receiving the gift and *she is*, I have to imagine what it might be like to be her. In doing so, I experience empathy.

23

Observations of behaviors can be utilized to *express* empathy: "You sound excited," or "It looks like you're feeling sad." When we perceive a feeling in another, expressing that can build connection *if we're right*. Stating what we see or hear is safe because the other person can correct us. "I'm not sad—I probably look that way because I'm exhausted." When we tell another they *are* feeling something, or that we can *understand* how they are feeling, we're in dangerous territory because it presupposes that we know.

In fact, we can never fully know or understand another's experience. When we listen deeply to another, we notice signs and signals that indicate how they're feeling. A person with a high degree of social awareness—the aspect of emotional intelligence defined by the ability to recognize the emotions of others—can pick up these signals and check them out by reflecting what they see or hear. While it's a skill that can be built, reducing this reflection behavior to a technique misses the importance. It can seem insincere if the listener does not know how to separate her own feelings and biases from the observations she's making.

What Empathy Is

Empathy occurs when we seek to see things from the experiential point of view of another. When we experience empathic feelings, we realize that the other's point of view is rationally consistent from his or her perspective, however disjointed it may appear from ours. Empathy does not mean we must agree or have positive feelings about the other's point of view. It's about using our good will to understand another, whether we agree with them or not.

—CATHERINE ANNE LOMBARD[11]

An exhibit in Europe's traveling Empathy Museum, entitled *A Mile in My Shoes*, allows visitors to literally do just that—walk in someone else's shoes. Their website says the exhibit "holds a diverse collection of shoes and audio stories that explore our shared humanity. From a Syrian refugee to a sex worker, a war veteran to a neurosurgeon, visitors are invited to walk a mile in the shoes of a stranger while listening to their story."[12]

While we can never really know what another is feeling or experiencing, we can come close by approximating their state of being. It begins with the physical body—our own. If we are to metaphorically step into another's shoes, we must first embody our own shoes in order to make the distinction. Then, we can observe ourselves from their perspective. Here's an example:

I'm planning a conversation with my colleague Tonya. Tonya recently had foot surgery and is still wearing a cast. Since the surgery, she has been working remotely, sharing a makeshift, spare-bedroom office with her remote-working husband and their new puppy. I've been getting increasingly frustrated during my conversations with Tonya. She has become quite negative and even sighs frequently. Yesterday she rolled her eyes on a Zoom call. It's not who she is, and I want to help her see how her behavior is affecting our entire team and their perception of her. Yet every conversation we have leaves the issue unresolved and seems to increase the tension between us.

To prepare for the conversation, I sit in my chair, in front of the screen I use to connect with Tonya on Zoom. I first notice my body: How am I sitting? Are my feet on the floor, sitz bones on the chair? No—and I feel that slight ache in my left knee. Imagining that I'm connecting with Tonya, I move my awareness to my upper body, then my face. I notice tension in my shoulders and tightness in my face. Am I really pursing my lips? As I look at her face on the imaginary screen, I begin to speak, and I listen to my tone. I begin to detect frustration—maybe even judgment. I take the time to examine the words I'm choosing. Then I identify the emotion I feel. It's more than frustration—it's exasperation, borne from the fact that I can't get through to this associate whom I admire so much. The exasperation lives in my shoulders and facial muscles. Could she be seeing that? Could she be put off by my tone of voice? I decide to check.

I now imagine myself in Tonya's spare bedroom. Momentarily "becoming" Tonya, I sit down in her chair and prop my foot onto the oversized ottoman. I adjust my body so my leg fits nearly parallel to the desk and the computer screen blocks the sun from the window. I notice that the cast is heavy. If I focus on it, I can feel the tight restriction it creates on my foot and ankle. In this odd position, I notice discomfort in my hip and back. I also notice what a challenge it is to make eye contact with the camera. Paying attention to the environment, I can hear my husband consumed by his work, talking as if I'm not there. As if this doesn't distract me enough, I can hear the incessant chewing of our puppy. While I love my puppy, the noise is driving me crazy. Now I look into the screen. I see my work colleague alone in her well-equipped private office. She looks tense. *What now?* I think. *Is she going to try to cheer me up or admonish me?* As she begins to talk, I realize it's the latter. She has no idea what I'm going through.

27

From this exercise, I get a glimpse into what Tonya is experiencing. While I don't know exactly what she's feeling—I can't label her emotions with precision, and I don't really know how her foot and body feel—what I gain is her experience of me, in the context of everything else she has going on. That precious information allows me to adjust my approach. I can sit differently, relax my shoulder and facial muscles, choose a different tone and perhaps different words. The empathy that I now have transforms my previous feeling of exasperation. It becomes compassion. I feel prepared for our next conversation and hopeful about its outcome.

People often ask me, "How do you know that Tonya will respond well to the new approach?" The answer is that while I don't know for sure *how* she will react, I do know that she will react differently, given that my approach will be vastly different. By identifying my own physical and emotional state of being, observing my colleague's, *and* deciding to choose a compassionate approach, my colleague's response is likely to be very different.

In their white paper *Empathy in the Workplace*, the Center for Creative Leadership points out that "having empathy is not the same as demonstrating empathy."[13] Displaying empathy is what I would call compassion. The leadership behaviors the authors of the white paper identify as demonstrating empathy include:

28

- Being sensitive to signs of overwork in others
- Showing interest in others' needs, hopes, and dreams
- Being willing to help others with personal problems.
- Expressing compassion when others share a personal loss

Grow Emotional Intelligence

Development is one of the essential practices for growing the inner qualities leaders need now. Developing compassion requires empathy, and we can learn to consciously direct our attention away from ourselves and perceive another to gain that empathy. Underlying that ability is a body of study called *emotional intelligence*, which is something that can be developed with intentional practice.

Numerous academic researchers have sought and found evidence that emotional intelligence is a marker of mental health, career success, positive relationships, and life satisfaction. But like most academic leadership theories, it too is fraught with debate because it's hard to measure and shaped by context. And, if context was a challenge pre-pandemic, it is certainly highlighted now, when the old constructs simply don't match the world in which we work and live.

Nonetheless, I am going to take a stand here and

say that human beings are emotional beings, and right now many are nervous, depressed, angry, and frustrated. Having "emotional intelligence" is essential for leadership success, and it is a foundational building block for empathy and compassion.

Two of the four skills that make up emotional intelligence, according to Travis Bradberry and Jeanne Greaves, are self-awareness and social awareness. Self-awareness, in this context according to Bradberry and Greaves, is the "ability to perceive your emotions in the moment and understand your tendencies across situations." Social awareness is the "ability to accurately pick up on emotions in other people and understand what is really going on with them."[14]

The example I gave in the previous section is a sophisticated yet relatively easy way to gain this self- and "other"-awareness. Reflecting on and making conscious our own behavior *and* acknowledging, even to ourselves, another's positive intent can shift our state of being from one of apathy, frustration, or even disdain to compassion. It's really that simple.

Self-Compassion

> *Self-compassion . . . requires that*
> *we recognize our own suffering.*
> —KRISTIN NEFF, PHD

Because work stress and work culture-induced stress and burnout are at all-time highs, leaders need compassion now more than ever. We have a profound responsibility. While employees at all levels enter employment agreements freely, employers make promises about cultural norms and expectations through values statements and other means. Post-pandemic, the rules are unpredictable. Understandably, organizations are trying to figure out what's best for their employees and customers. Compassion must be part of the leader's consideration.

Conversely, we all have responsibility for what we are willing to subject ourselves to. When individuals lack self-compassion, they fall prey to toxic cultures that demand more than they have to give. From my vantage point as a coach, it's often like watching a perfect storm. Those who have difficulty setting boundaries for what they will endure are often the most likely to be complicit with cultures that take advantage of their vulnerabilities. Consider the perfectionistic, *summa cum laude* Harvard Law graduate who works for a tyrannical law partner, or the hesitant worrier who works in a command-and-control, hierarchical organization.

None of us escape our history. Regardless of how loving and stable our upbringing (or how traumatic), we are products of our past. Leaders who have managed to live an unexamined life, and as Richard Rohr says, have "cultivated and protected a chosen persona,"[15] are often trapped inside an idea of themselves that does not match their true selves.

Three of these distinct personas, or archetypes as I'll call them here, are common to leaders I encounter in my work as an executive coach. They also align with the negative constructs Dr. Kristin Neff describes in the components of self-compassion.[16] These leaders include:

- *The Self-Critic:* Individuals who are overly self-critical, judging their own shortcomings more harshly than they would a friend's or a colleague's

- *The Perfectionist:* Individuals who are perfectionistic, irrationally thinking or acting as if human fallibility does not apply to them

- *The Ruminator:* Individuals who overidentify with, and ruminate over, negative thoughts and feelings, sometimes to the point of inaction or physical illness

The Self-Critic

> *. . . happiness*
> *might just*
> *be a single step away,*
> *on the other side*
> *of that next*
> *unhelpful*
> *and undeserving*
> *thought.*
>
> —DAVID WHYTE[17]

Self-critical individuals carry the weight of the world on their shoulders. They blame themselves when things go wrong, and their self-talk is often unkind.

Self-critics can be easy to spot because their self-deprecating self-talk almost always speaks out loud from time to time. But they might not even be aware of this part of themselves until someone points it out. This was surely true for me.

I consider myself accomplished in the kitchen. I'm skilled and creative with many types of food and receive compliments that reinforce that belief. So, imagine my shock when a friend, also a colleague who knows a thing or two about human psychology, pointed out the fact that I routinely negate or refuse compliments about my cooking and even criticize it in advance of serving it.

My friend offered this feedback, with evidence, at the end of a long weekend at my home, one in which I had enjoyed my usual pastime of treating guests to culinary delights served in a casual and inviting environment.

I had no idea that each time I served a meal or a snack, I qualified it with something like "I'm sorry that the muffins have only two types of berries. I didn't get to the market in time to get organic raspberries" or "Sadly, I let the edge of the crust get a bit too brown."

I was truly aghast at this observation. I really do believe I'm a talented cook and worthy of compliments. And I could see how unattractive it is to serve a beautiful meal with a portion of detritus.

"Why do I do this?" I asked myself.

As you might guess, my self-judgment shows up in places other than the kitchen. The question, "Why do I do this?" began a multiyear development journey to quiet my inner critic. Yet the deeper work, the transformational work, has been learning to *acknowledge* the part of me that critic judges so harshly, as I seek to treat her as I might a friend or a colleague who burned the potatoes or forgot to set their alarm. That is self-compassion— being kind and understanding toward oneself rather than being self-critical.

The Perfectionist

In order to unfold, self-compassion depends on honest, direct contact with our own vulnerability. This compassion fully blossoms when we actively offer care to ourselves.

—TARA BRACH[18]

According to Kristin Neff, "Perfectionism is defined as the compulsive need to accomplish one's goals with no allowance for falling short of one's ideals. Perfectionists experience enormous stress and anxiety about getting things right and feel devastated when they don't."[19]

There is a wide range of healthy and unhealthy traits that describe perfectionism, and I am not attempting to define it here in a way that is comprehensive. My purpose in this book is to suggest *what leaders need now.* And I believe that perfectionistic leaders need to give themselves a break, a show of self-compassion. Consider these classic perfectionists (you might relate to one or more of them):

- The leader who spends an inordinate amount of time wording and rewording emails to those in positions of authority
- The leader who makes a mistake and loses

hours or days lost in thoughts and feelings of failure and worthlessness
- The leader who cannot delegate, or delegates yet micromanages a project from start to finish
- The leader who criticizes others harshly

While perfectionists are self-critical, this archetype is distinct from the one I described previously in my cooking example. Perfectionists feel isolated when they fail, as if they are the only ones suffering or making mistakes. Seeing one's fallibility as being part of the larger human condition rather than as isolating is an opportunity for self-compassion.

The Ruminator

People who master [detachment] do two things well. First, they find ways to keep things in perspective. Second, they don't personalize things which don't belong to them.

—NICK PETRIE[20]

Researchers say we spend up to 70 percent of our waking time in a state of non-presence, thinking about the past or future. When we attach negative emotion to those thoughts, resilience expert Nick Petrie calls them "ruminations."

Ellen's eighteen-month tenure on the job has been filled with myriad accomplishments, milestones never previously met by the organization.

Three months ago, she was given an additional responsibility, and three weeks ago, she received a stellar performance review, indicating that she had exceeded expectations. Near the end of a recent week, she received a meeting request to meet with her leader and her leader's boss, the company president, the following Monday morning. Ellen spent the weekend ruminating, and by Monday morning, she was sure this meeting was set to reprimand her at best and, at worst, to terminate her. Of course, neither happened. Instead she was offered a promotion.

Bob is an executive in a very toxic culture that is becoming increasingly unhealthy physically and mentally. He is mid-career in a high-demand field and is able to relocate. He has always made financial security a priority and has ample living expenses readily available in addition to retirement savings. Bob admits to spending nearly every spare moment worrying about getting fired or resigning from his job. He feels shame about it all and ruminates over what friends, family, and future employers will think. This has all but paralyzed him from being proactive about searching for a new role elsewhere.

When we catastrophize, we are unkind to ourselves. Holding our painful thoughts and feelings in mindful awareness—rather than avoiding or overidentifying with them—is another form of self-compassion. The leaders I describe here overidentify with their thoughts and feelings to the point of coming to irrational conclusions. And they also waste precious time in their minds, time that can be spent enjoying time with loved ones or doing meaningful work.

Since that moment in my kitchen so many years ago, my self-critic has been the subject of personal reflection as well as formal development with my coaches and mentors. If you relate to one or more of the three archetypes—the self-critic, the perfectionist, or the ruminator—the essential practices of development, reflection, and acknowledgment are key to developing self-compassion. The reward is great. And while the evidence of a link between a leader who displays self-compassion and compassion for others is limited, the behaviors—validation, acceptance, and kindness, for example—are very much the same. In a work world where stress and anxiety have reached epidemic highs, we need more leaders aware of their capacity for—or lack of—compassion for themselves, and for others.

Time to Reflect

1. What did you agree with strongly, and/or disagree with strongly?
2. What evoked an emotional response, and possibly even suggested an area of personal vulnerability?
3. What one thing calls you to act, from a development perspective?

THREE

The Context for Courage

Courage has always been at the heart of leadership, for without it there would be no "leading"; there would only be a stuck-ness in how things are and should stay. Yet one can "lead astray," "lead on" (in the sense of deceit), and lead others in a way that is self-serving and harmful. It takes much courage to lead toward a greater good, a selfless cause, or a just end.

In this chapter, I define why leaders need courage more than ever before—why it is one of the qualities leaders need now. First, let's not be confused about what courage really is. Once again, context is essential for defining the essential qualities, and this is certainly true for courage. There are a multitude of behaviors that in one context represent courage and in another do not. Courage is not saying any old thing that pops into your mind. Sharing unwelcome feedback inappropriately, for example, can be cruel, not courageous. Courage is not fearlessness; fearlessness can be foolishness. Leaders can confuse courage with promoting unsafe or unnecessary risks. Enduring untenable circumstances can look heroic yet be more martyr-like than courageous. The list goes on.

The Courage to Transform Oneself

Distinguished authors and leadership researchers Jim Kouzes and Barry Posner note that while courage is often touted as a leadership quality, there is very little discussion of courage in leadership literature. Their brief work, *Finding the Courage to Lead*, is a result of their research on courageous leadership.

Kouzes and Posner note that "challenges call forth courage." Their research parallels my experience with courageous decisions leaders make every day:

[The challenges] were about, for instance, leaving a comfortable job to start a new business, about having to perform for the first time in public, about completely changing careers when everyone else advised against it, about blowing the whistle on a colleague, about revealing something intensely personal that could jeopardize a job and risk lifelong friendships, about standing up to authority, and about having to fire a very close friend.[21]

When faced with adversity, we have three choices. We can avoid, endure, or transform. In the examples Kouzes and Posner listed here, the leader faces these choices. One choice is to *avoid* a transformational opportunity—for example, leaving one job in a state of blame only to have the same problem show up in the next, or pretending to live a very different life than one does in order to be accepted and avoid judgment. The other choice is to *endure* the current situation—stay stuck in a job you loathe because of the security it provides, or openly share your personal values in an environment that is persecutorial. The courageous choice always involves transformation. Here is an example:

> Over the span of a career, few leaders escape the difficult task of reorganizing and resizing their teams. Joi, an executive leader, recently had to make a difficult decision, one impacting a tenured employee for whom she cared deeply and had supported for many years. This can be done in a humane or inhumane way, and this organization puts people first. Still, Joi was troubled by the decision. She could have avoided it and chosen another way to reduce payroll costs. She knew the right thing to do was to exit the individual no longer capable of performing the job, even though

he was a loyal friend and colleague. The courage Joi displayed with her decision was not simply a matter of mustering the gumption to act. While it sounds paradoxical, she had to let go of her self-consciousness and need for acceptance and instead focus on compassion for the individual and the rest of the team. It required a personal shift that was transformational. She did the right thing, not the easy thing.

Part of Kouzes' and Posner's research involved asking people to recount stories of personal courage. Among others, they noted a critical, common factor: Taking courageous action is transformational.

> After telling us their moment-of-courage stories, people related how their lives were never the same after they'd chosen to act. Courage wasn't a word used to describe every challenging experience or every situation that demanded change. It was reserved for those that were liberating and transformative.[22]

As I was writing this chapter, I reached out to my colleagues for a story in which a leader "spoke truth to power." Dianne Earley of D. Earley Coaching and Consulting provided this:

My client's company suffered a significant blow to its payroll infrastructure, which caused some hourly wage team members to be paid incorrectly. There was an immediate and clear focus on solving the issue, but the problem droned on for weeks. During that time, concerns escalated for team members, as did their questions and complaints.

From the perspective of many of the company's senior-level executives, minimizing the financial and legal impact on the company and reducing the number and scope of affected employees was the goal, and resources were poured in that direction. They expected the impacted workers to understand and appreciate the efforts underway.

Comments like these were overheard from well-meaning leaders who were trying to calm the fray:

"Don't worry, the problem is being addressed. Just trust us."

"We are doing the best we can, but this problem is out of our control."

"Just be patient. This will all be corrected by the next pay period."

When their responses weren't received in the way they hoped they would be, some leaders stopped communicating altogether. Many team members began to feel that the payroll issue was being trivialized, and frustration skyrocketed.

During an executive team meeting, leaders were asked to report on the feedback they were receiving from their frontline workers about the problem. Many shared stories of ongoing complaints, increasing disengagement, and waning job performance. Their team members seemed hyper-focused on the short-term payroll issue, even though promises were made to make everyone whole as quickly as possible. They were losing trust in their team members' ability to deliver business results in the meantime. Nods of agreement and looks of exasperation were shared around the room. One leader decided to provide the clarity and empathy that was needed in that moment . . . and it went like this:

"Our coworkers have every right to feel frustrated and angry," she said. "We have marginalized them by refusing to look at this issue from their perspective. Any one of us [leaders] can wait for another pay period or another month or probably longer for an issue like this to be corrected without missing a beat. But we need to understand that many of our hourly wage coworkers are literally living from paycheck to paycheck. Waiting one more pay period to receive the money they are due creates real hardships that no one in this meeting has to deal with. And

46

suggesting that they patiently wait until we solve a problem that is literally disrupting the lives of their families demonstrates our inability as a leadership team to connect to the people who drive the success of our business. And it is insulting. At a minimum, we owe them communication, even if we don't have all the answers. We have to take ownership to earn trust. Can we put ourselves in their shoes for just one minute?"

Silence followed first. But in that minute, they all got it. And the conversations with team members the next day, and the day after, and the day after that, were amazingly, authentically different—as was the urgency to remediate the situation. The leader that defied executive group-think to share a different perspective exemplified the courage that leaders need now.

The Courage to Transform Organizations

Some years ago, I authored a popular learning program entitled Courageous Conversations. Its goal was to help leaders and their teams listen to understand one another, engage in truth-telling, and exchange respectful, candid feedback. Its purpose was to enhance trust and productivity. When you increase trust, so the research goes, you increase productivity.

I built the Courageous Conversations program in

the era of the popularity of bestsellers such as *Crucial Conversations* and *Fierce Conversations*. I think of this time as the first wave of a movement that operationalized the early dialogue work of Chris Argyris and later the systems thinking work of Peter Senge. It was followed by a second wave, what I'll call the "vulnerability era," introduced by Brené Brown with her blockbuster TED Talk "The Power of Vulnerability." That talk, now viewed over 67 million times, launched her immense success and popularity. Her work continues to give so many the freedom that results from authenticity.

In her book *Gifts of Imperfection*, Brown links courage with vulnerability:

> The root of the word courage is *cor* – the Latin word for heart. In one of its earliest forms, the word courage had a very different definition than it does today. Courage originally meant "To speak one's mind by telling all one's heart."
>
> Over time, this definition has changed, and today, courage is more synonymous with being heroic. Heroics is important and we certainly need heroes, but I think we've lost touch with the idea that speaking honestly and openly about who we are, about what we're feeling, and about our experiences (good and bad) is the definition of courage.
>
> Heroics is often about putting our life on

the line. Ordinary courage is about putting our vulnerability on the line.[23]

Being able to speak honestly about who we are and share our feelings and experiences is highlighted as an essential element in everything from high-trust teams to inclusive workplaces. We all need skills and the support of learning programs to do this well, as well as the self-awareness and willingness to display courageous vulnerability. But the fact remains: We are not always safe. That's why leaders need courage now. Many of the fundamental underpinnings of our organizations and institutions do not support courageous vulnerability, however. What we need now are leaders who are courageous enough to change culture at its core.

In his *HBR* article, "What Courageous Leaders Do Differently," James R. Detert says:

In the vast majority of organizations, entreating people to routinely stick their necks out despite legitimate fear isn't exactly a sign of strong leadership. Yet that's what leaders who "encourage courage" are essentially doing. They're implicitly saying that because *they* aren't courageous enough to change the conditions in their organization to make it safer for people to be honest, try new things, or take other prudent risks, everyone else should be courageous enough to do them anyway.[24]

Would-be courageous leaders are often halted by their own survival fears. Rare are leaders who risk their own careers when taking courageous action might carry that cost. I recall one colleague who took such a risk several years ago.

Leah had mentored a team member, Alonzo, for two years and had grown to trust him and his abilities. He had great instincts and raw talent. When she was promoted and needed to name a successor, she recommended him for the role, even though he lacked formal education and what we would label "executive presence" today. Leah knew she could help him develop the skills and capabilities he needed and believed that his potential for future growth at their firm was great. When she presented the idea to her boss, he responded with three words: "It's your neck." Leah had the courage to "stick her neck out." She knew that her leader did not support her decision, but she trusted herself—and Alonzo. As it turned out, Alonzo excelled in that role—and was promoted again to an organizational leadership role a few years later. Leah describes him today as one of the best leaders she has ever worked with. She was willing to take responsibility for what she thought was the right decision, even if it jeopardized her own career. While Leah's action was admirable, she was alone without support. Many middle managers would not have taken that risk.

An easy-to-spot place where courage is encouraged yet responsibility is sometimes abdicated to others is when the list of behavioral norms, guiding principles, or core values doesn't apply to top leaders. Adherence to guiding principles takes courage, and they are dangerous if the unwritten, institutional norms don't support them. For example, consider the two behavior groups that Detert names: 1) open, transparent communication and 2) innovation and risk-taking. It's irresponsible for leaders to tout these as behavioral expectations if there are unaddressed historical and cultural practices that reward the opposite and punish the new. Yet we see it every day.

In my work as a coach, the barriers to advancing culture change almost always involve the behavior of leaders at multiple levels. Courageous leaders take on these behavior issues, which include everything from disrespectful communication to abusive work conditions. They address them, work to change them, and most importantly, make it clear they won't be tolerated. They prioritize the people-interaction aspect of leadership by making sure it's highlighted, and they don't hide behind lack of awareness until an issue is escalated to Human Resources. These leaders are courageous enough to sacrifice the business value of a leader if that leader's behavior is counter to the values of the organization.

I have had so many conversations with executives who agonize over what becomes a very real ethical dilemma around courage when considering the termination of employees for (ongoing) violation of company behavior norms and values. There are significant business risks to losing key employees, from simple productivity at an inconvenient time to potentially crippling loss of major accounts, proprietary knowledge, and difficult-to-replace talent. But the alternative—turning a blind eye—risks cultural integrity. Other members of the organization see the behaviors being tolerated, even rewarded, and conclude that so-called organizational values are only words on paper.

Another courage-encouragement danger zone involves diversity, equity, and inclusion (DEI) strategies. It takes hard work on the part of top leaders to ensure these strategies come to fruition. The 2020 Catalyst white paper, *Getting Real About Inclusive*

Leadership, named six core behaviors essential to being an inclusive leader. Courage is one, and the authors define it this way: "You act in accordance with your principles, even when it involves personal risk-taking or is uncomfortable."[25] Unfortunately, one of the ways some mid-level leaders act in accordance with their principles is to leave. While this can be a transformational act of personal courage, these leaders often leave because the risk of exposing the lack of inclusion in their environment is too great. Others test the safety of speaking truth to power and find that their messages are heard and heeded, creating progress.

Organizational change occurs due to both kinds of individual courageous acts: exiting on principle as well as risky grassroots efforts to raise issues and thus initiate change. Yet there is a dimension of leadership courage set aside for executives with the positional authority to change the institution at its core. These leaders walk their talk and live their values even when it's hard. Hard, at the executive level, means taking risks in the marketplace and with one's own political capital. Perhaps another reason acting with this level of courage is hard is that leaders must *believe in* whatever principle they are being asked to take a stand on. David Whyte says:

To be courageous is to seat our feelings deeply
in the body and in the world: to live up to and into
the necessities of relationships that already exist,
with things we find we already care deeply about:
a person, a future, a possibility in society or with an
unknown that begs on us—and has always begged
on us. To be courageous is to stay close to the way
we are made.[26]

Dinesh C. Paliwal, former president and CEO of
Harman and now partner at KKR Private Equity, is one
executive leader who represents courageous change
in the DEI arena.

The global conversation about diversity and
inclusion is changing. It's getting louder. The push
for racial, ethnic, and gender equality is now top
of mind for business leaders around the world.
And yet, talk has not always led to action. A fear
of being uncomfortable has led to a misguided
mindset—an avoidance of difficult conversations
and concrete action—in the workplace. That needs
to change. And change starts at the top.[27]

Paliwal doesn't talk—he acts. Of his efforts at
Harman, he says:

Diversifying our organization across gender, geography, culture, age and experience has been the single most valuable component of Harman's transformation and success over the past 10 years. Simply put, diverse teams perform better.[28]

The Call to Courage, Now

Making work environments—whether remote or office-based—places where people thrive on creativity, are engaged in meaningful, purposeful work, feel supported and appreciated, and can be fully welcomed for their uniqueness is the intent of most enlightened leaders today. While some organizations achieve this, many do not. Throughout this book, I have pointed to the increasing levels of stress employees at all levels are experiencing, and I have also pointed to the fact that despite decades of attempts at remediation, many organizations accept behaviors that range from subtle bias to bullying and abuse.

My act of courage is to speak this truth. In my work, I am privileged to witness vast talent, intellect, and insight. I work with people who care immensely about the people they lead, their organizations' purpose, and the customers and shareholders they serve. I've also had a unique lens to witness the pain and suffering that result from inappropriate, disrespectful, and even inhumane behavior in the workplace. This is not a specific indictment of any leader; these behaviors can be unintentional and unconscious. Yet those leaders who have the awareness hold the responsibility.

I make a distinction between taking a personally courageous action that impacts oneself and perhaps a small circle of others, and the kind of courageous action that organizational leaders with the positional authority sufficient to make sweeping culture change can affect. Only you know what you are willing and able to do, and what your span of influence holds.

Time to Reflect

1. What did you agree with strongly, and/or disagree with strongly?
2. What evoked an emotional response, and possibly even suggested an area of personal vulnerability?
3. What one thing calls you to act, from a development perspective?

FOUR

The Hidden Gifts of Humility

Are you feeling a bit on edge beginning this chapter? *Humility* is simply not a word we commonly use outside of spiritual contexts, even though much has been written in leadership texts about related concepts: servant leadership, vulnerability, and beginner's mind, to name a few examples.

I've been working to articulate, beyond instinct alone, why leaders need humility now more than ever. Ironically, it takes humility to understand the claim. If you believe, as I do, that we are living in a world of profound uncertainty in which many of the norms and principles that worked just fine in the past no longer serve us, that we cannot rely on what we have always believed to be true, and that our vulnerability requires the support of community, then you are already embracing the nature of humility.

Consider that the root of the word *humble* is *humus*, meaning "earth." Humus is the organic matter in soil that improves plant fertility, as well as resistance to drought and disease. Imagine, as you read the pages that follow, an earthy richness to be gained from exploring the nature of humility as it relates to your leadership. I most definitely gained new perspective from researching and writing this chapter.

Humility, Gratitude, and Control

Humility is a portal to deeper and more abiding gratitude. And yet, humility is not a word most of us are fully comfortable with, if we attach to the concept that we are, or must remain, in control. Humility is rooted in the relationship of both giver and receiver.

—COLETTE LAFIA[29]

A few weeks ago, on the Wednesday before Thanksgiving, I drove forty miles "over the hill," as we call it, to Trader Joe's. That was probably not the best choice of days for grocery shopping, but I had an open afternoon and plenty of time. Mindful of not getting stressed by the crowds or lack of items on the shelves, I filled my cart with things we needed and headed to the checkout line. They're very efficient at Trader Joe's, and half of my order had been processed by the time I opened my handbag to retrieve my wallet.

It wasn't there.

As a feeling of dread rushed over me, I frantically searched my bag for anything that might help and found that I had fifty dollars in cash and an out-of-state business check (but no identification to prove it was mine). Feeling embarrassed, I offered this to the kind clerk and asked if I might check my car to see if my wallet was there. She said, "Yes, of course," and said she would ask the manager about accepting my check in the meantime.

The wallet was not in my car. I realized it was likely sitting on my desk, where I mindlessly placed it after removing it from my backpack after walking the dog. I reentered the store, quite settled with the notion that if they would not accept my check, I would leave the groceries, go home to get my wallet, and return.

When I reached the checkout counter and began to speak, the clerk interrupted me. "I have it all worked out," she said. "We cannot accept out-of-state checks. But I'm going to pay for your groceries, and you can pay me back the next time you're in. You can pay the fifty dollars in cash you have, and I'll put the rest on my credit card."

I opened my mouth to protest, and she said, "I want to do this for Thanksgiving. I want to do something kind, and this is it. And I'm going off shift now and will be on vacation over the holiday, so don't come back right away. Don't waste gas; come when you need to be in the area again."

In that moment of truth, by some grace that I usually do not possess, I said, "Thank you." My mind said otherwise. My mind said I could put back all but fifty dollars' worth of items. I could return with payment that afternoon. I hesitate to admit it, but I did not want to accept her kindness with unqualified gratitude. My ego-laden mind wanted to be in control, and needing help was not part of the program. Yet in that moment, my heart answered, not my ego. I allowed myself to transform what would have been a stressful afternoon into one of grace and ease.

As I drove home, I thought of this chapter on humility, and the seeming connection between gratitude and humility. To be grateful means we must accept the kindness of another or the good fortune that arises from an answered prayer, a successful endeavor, or a vision realized. One of humility's characteristics is valuing others. Gratitude is a felt sense of having benefited from the actions of another. Deb, the clerk at Trader Joe's, had the desire to extend a kindness at Thanksgiving. What she gave me was the gift of a *state* of thanksgiving in my heart in response to her generosity. Once I was able to detach from my ego's interference, I was able to appreciate not only the gesture, but also the fact that there are generous and trusting people among us.

As it turns out, the evidence extends beyond my trip to Trader Joe's:

In two experiments and one diary study, we examined the relationship between self- and other-oriented processes by considering how gratitude can influence humility and vice versa. Humility is characterized by low self-focus, secure sense of self, and increased valuation of others. Gratitude is marked by a sense that one has benefited from the actions of another. In the first experiment, participants who wrote a gratitude letter showed higher state humility than those who performed a neutral activity. In the second experiment, baseline state humility predicted the amount of gratitude felt after writing a gratitude letter compared to a neutral activity. Finally, in a 14-day diary study, humility and gratitude mutually predicted one another, even after controlling for the other's prior level. Our results suggest that humility and gratitude are mutually reinforcing.[30]

Confident Humility

Confident Humility: Having faith in our capability while appreciating that we may not have the right solution or even be addressing the right problem.

—ADAM GRANT[31]

Many thought leaders point out that we often mistakenly consider humility to be a quality on one end of a continuum, with traits like power, confidence, and assuredness on the other. Adam Grant makes this point clearly in his book *Think Again*:

Many people picture confidence as a seesaw. Gain too much confidence and we tip toward arrogance. Lose too much confidence and we become meek. This is our fear with humility: that we'll end up having a low opinion of ourselves.[32]

He goes on to say:

Humility is often misunderstood. It is not a matter of low self-confidence. . . . You can be confident in your ability to achieve a goal in the future while maintaining the humility to question whether you have the right tools in the present.[33]

Tim Burkett, Guiding Teacher at the Minnesota Zen Meditation Center, says something similar:

The more naturally humble you are the more confident you are. It's not a childish, arrogant confidence that is based on some accomplishment that you are proud of. Relaxed confidence doesn't depend on accomplishment because it is the parent of accomplishment not the child of it.

You don't have to be right all the time. If you worry about being right then you have a very fragile confidence. But with humility your confidence is steady, it can withstand turbulent times when things don't go the way you thought they would. When you fall down you just get up. Falling down is no problem. Asking for help is no problem.[34]

I dream of a day when Burkett's sentiment is widely accepted in the workplace. Why do we still believe leaders have to have all the answers? The very idea seems to define arrogance, yet it is often an expectation we have of those we interact with. Not many would disagree that organizations must constantly transform to remain relevant; in fact, it's that premise that is foundational to the 1990s theory of organizational learning—the idea that whole cultures must be focused on ongoing inquiry, growth, and change, not mere training of individuals. Yet hubris still prevails, and it stands in the way of the learning that is necessary for innovation and marketplace success.

In the beginner's mind there are many possibilities, but in the expert's there are few.

—SHUNRYU SUZUKI ROSHI[35]

Recently a senior executive, Joseph, asked me to work with Devon, one of his leaders, on his ability to communicate business issues clearly. Joseph wants Devon, the more junior leader, to understand that he (Joseph) does not always understand the context of the issues Devon is presenting. Joseph wants Devon to *ask* him if he needs more detail or context versus presuming he *knows everything* by virtue of his title and position. When I relayed this feedback to Devon, he was a bit taken aback, as presuming senior leaders have all the knowledge and all of the answers is a cultural norm in that organization, albeit one they are working to change.

Modern-Day Servant Leadership

Humility must never be confused with meekness. Humility is being open to the ideas of others.

—SIMON SINEK

Even though humility is not yet a popular word in many organizations, evidence abounds of the seminal nature of Robert Greenleaf's 1970 essay "The Servant as Leader" and his subsequent work. Greenleaf died in 1990, yet his work lives on through The Greenleaf Center for Servant Leadership. It's easy to find well-known leadership experts' views on this concept. Marshall Goldsmith, Brené Brown, Stephen M.R. Covey, Jim Kouzes, Simon Sinek, and Cheryl Bachelder all weigh in with essays in Ken Blanchard's book, *Servant Leadership in Action*.

Dan Cable, professor of organizational behavior at London Business School, presents a succinct modern-day summary of servant leadership in his *HBR* article, "How Humble Leadership Really Works."

Top-down leadership is outdated and counterproductive. By focusing too much on control and end goals, and not enough on their people, leaders are making it more difficult to achieve their own desired outcomes. The key, then, is to help people feel purposeful, motivated, and energized so they can bring their best selves to work.

One of the best ways is to adopt the humble mind-set of a servant leader. Servant leaders view their key role as serving employees as they explore and grow, providing tangible and emotional support as they do so.

To put it bluntly, servant-leaders have the

humility, courage, and insight to admit that they can benefit from the expertise of others who have less power than them.[36]

Evidence is also emerging to support the positive impact of servant leadership on team performance and business outcomes.

Shelby Scarbrough, author of *Civility Rules!*, is an advocate for humility as a trademark of effective leaders. In a recent *Forbes* article, she names a study by a team from Arizona State University and the National University of Singapore showing that "humble CEOs (defined as those who recognized their own strengths and weaknesses and appreciated the strengths and contributions of others) often created better financial returns for their companies. The study, published in the *Journal of Management*, identified a connection between humility in the CEO and greater collaboration in the C-suite, as well as better decision-making at all levels."[37]

Here are a few highlights of the research Adam Grant cites on the case for humble leaders:[38]

- Students can significantly improve their willingness to seek extra help when presented with the benefits of admitting what we don't know.
- Students who admit they don't know

something and are willing to revise their beliefs get higher grades than their self-assured peers.

- Studies show the most productive and innovative teams are run by leaders who score high in both confidence and humility.
- The most skilled—and successful—negotiators bring a "scientist's level of humility and curiosity" to the table.

Why is there such a gap between the evidence that servant leadership, rooted in humility, results in purposeful, motivated individuals and innovative, productive teams and the absence of the behaviors that support it in day-to-day organizational life?

For the answer, I hearken back to my encounter at Trader Joe's and the "moment of truth" in which my heart and mind were in a standoff. Ego is one of the culprits. Ken Blanchard, in a *Forbes* interview about his book, *Servant Leadership in Action*, describes the dichotomy at play.

Ego interferes with effective leadership in two ways: one is false pride—thinking *more* of yourself than you should. You push and shove for credit and spend a lot of time promoting yourself. The other way is self-doubt or fear—thinking less of yourself than you should. You're consumed with your own shortcomings and spend a lot of time protecting yourself.[39]

In my work as a coach, I often see one or the other displacing heartfelt service to others.

Adam Grant says: "People gain humility when they reflect on how different circumstances could have led them to different beliefs."[40] I'm reminded of the example of "stepping into Tonya's shoes" in Chapter Two, and how that exercise can shift one's beliefs. It requires suspension of the ego to do so. It's a way of taking an alternate position to the "self," whether the self that is showing up in the moment is self-pride or self-doubt, as Blanchard defines them.

The Freedom of Humility

"Not knowing for sure" is a famous Zen practice—it conveys the truth of our human incarnation. Not knowing and acting anyway, with a playful and caring heart, you cede control of the outcome and willingly cast your unique spirit into the mystery.

—JACK KORNFIELD

In my experience, it takes a certain degree of humility

to accept failure, whether that failure results from a promising experiment or an unplanned error. Perfectionists, or anyone who likes to maintain a strong sense of control, can struggle with this. Yet we know that admitting mistakes builds trust rather than erodes it, and promising failures are the seeds of innovation.

There is freedom inherent in being able to let go of the need to always have the answers, make the right decisions, and instead, become open to the creativity, wisdom, and gifts of others. The freedom of a whole new world opens up for leaders who have not actively practiced humility, for when they shift from the ego-self to the "other," many other essential inner qualities become accessible, including compassion and courage. In the upcoming final chapter, we will look at practical ways to access these qualities.

Time to Reflect
1. What did you agree with strongly, and/or disagree with strongly?
2. What evoked an emotional response, and possibly even suggested an area of personal vulnerability?
3. What one thing calls you to act, from a development perspective?

FIVE

The Practices

Start close in,
don't take the second step
or the third,
start with the first
thing
close in,
the step
you don't want to take.

—DAVID WHYTE[41]

At this point in the reading of this short book, you might share my belief that the qualities of compassion, courage, and humility are essential for leaders now. It's my hope that there is something compelling here for you personally—either a desire to build and strengthen the qualities within yourself or to create a team, organization, or community in which they are represented more fully. Whichever it is, if you were to ask me where to begin, I would always, always say: "Start with yourself." If you are a leader with great compassion and want to expand your organization's efforts to nurture your employees' well-being, does that require courage on your part? If you consider yourself a humble servant leader, do you possess the *confident humility* Adam Grant writes about?

As you reflected on the questions at the end of each chapter, did you identify any vulnerabilities, any areas that suggested a thus-far unexamined part of your makeup? You see where I am going here: Leadership begins with you. It always does. And sometimes it's the step you don't want to take.

In my work, I am privileged to meet leaders at all stages of their development journey. One group of individuals are those who, until circumstances made their acquaintance, did not appear to know they were on a development journey. Life, including work, just "worked"—until it didn't. They were doing just fine (or so they thought) until external situations provided a proverbial knock on the door, indicating a need to acknowledge what manifested as a habit or behavior that was either no longer tolerable to others around them or derailed their forward career progression. Some of these individuals ignore the knock for a time, others answer the door and fight the messenger, while still others heed the call, embracing it wholeheartedly, thus opening a whole new world of personal discovery.

Another group of leaders appear to be natural lifelong learners. These individuals embrace self-development as if it's as essential as water and sleep. They have participated in a wide variety of developmental modalities, often including therapy. They willingly take advantage of programs, workshops, and seminars offered in work and personal settings. Not surprisingly, these leaders sponsor and support others to have the same opportunities.

Here's what I have learned from nearly twenty years as an executive coach: No one is "born" driven toward self-development. We make a decision to become conscious of the culture, conditioning, and experiences, positive and traumatic, that make us who we are today. As Richard Rohr expressed so well, we cannot plan our own enlightenment. The leader who truly welcomes personal development and is committed to coaching and mentoring others usually has a reason for doing so. That reason provides the impetus for growth into one's best and most purposeful self.

As a coach, I've worked with one individual, a lifelong learner-type, who decided to transform his life in grade school (I was lucky enough to meet him in his forties), and I've also worked with others who did not begin looking inward until their sixties. It really does not matter when you begin. If you've begun, continue. If you feel self-aware, evolved, self-actualized, and mature, dig deeper—and then deeper. Why? Because the leader your team, your family, and the world needs now is the authentic you, not the conditioning you've had, the stories you've told yourself (or been told), or the wounds you've endured. The practices of acknowledgment, reflection, and development are lifelong ways of being for all who embrace lifelong learning.

My purpose in this chapter is not to give you more tools for building compassion, courage, and humility. Rather, my hope is that the practices of development, reflection, and acknowledgment will remind you that growth as a leader is a journey, one that is filled with the creative discovery of your vision and purpose.

The Leadership Development Cycle
On their own, the three practices of development, reflection, and acknowledgment have broad definitions. Let's define them in the context of what I will call "the simple leadership development cycle."

Acknowledge

Develop   Reflect

Which comes first? That question is unanswerable. The limitation of the graphic on the previous page is that it appears static. Imagine it instead in constant, cyclical motion. Growth as a leader, then, is an ongoing cycle of self-discovery and intentional action. There is no prescribed starting point and no set sequence.

Development

Development is the process by which we cast a vision for the future that is congruent with our true nature and desires, and in doing so, identify and work through the personal stops along the way.

Throughout the development journey, we make conscious the unconscious patterns and habits that have formed over a lifetime, examine and assess their effectiveness in our current life, and act intentionally to transform that which no longer serves our vision and purpose.

If development is a journey, then vision and purpose—the destination—is the work of leaders. The work is the journey. I believe that, at any given stage of our development, we have a growing edge, a yet unexamined place of vulnerability that holds a key to our next leap or our next baby step. Carl Jung said, "Everyone carries a shadow, and the less it is embodied in the individual's conscious life, the blacker and denser it is."[42] Richard Rohr says, "The shadow is what you refuse to see about yourself, and what you do not want others to see."[43] The irony, as he points out, is that everyone but you usually sees it. By acknowledging it, you become free. That is a natural part of the development journey.

How one proceeds doesn't matter, as long as there is a how. For one of my colleagues, practice takes the form of quarterly silent retreats in a secluded monastery surrounded by a pristine mountain forest where she writes and meditates. For many leaders, practice involves working with a coach, a mentor, a counselor, or some combination of those. A development practice can include self-study as well as formal facilitator-led workshops and retreats. If you don't have a practice, you are not practicing.

Reflection

Reflection, in the context of this work, consists of self-reflection, the process of observing and assessing our thoughts, feelings, and behavior, and the reasons behind them as well as consideration of perspective surrounding external circumstances impacting us and those we impact and influence. Reflection is integral to learning. It brings forth self-awareness and builds consciousness.

Reading this definition of reflection, it sounds as if it could cure the world's ills, and it possibly could. There is a small problem, though. Thinking is dangerous when left to one's own mind. Reflection can easily be confused with rumination, the process by which we solidify our obsessions rather than gain perspective on them.

Still, reflection is essential. Dr. Geil Browning, founder of Emergenetics International, cites research showing that call center employees "who spent 15 minutes considering the lessons learned from the day performed 23 percent better than those that did not."[44]

Michelle Hlubinka of the MIT Media Lab says:

> The process of reflection helps us to develop
> our understanding more deeply and to make
> our intuitive knowledge shareable with others. It
> provides the opportunity to step back and take
> a look at what our work means to us and our
> communities.[45]

In my experience working with hundreds of clients, those who take time to consciously reflect on the insights they gain and the accomplishments they achieve during our engagement are much more likely to continue the learning process. Reflection allows us to sort successes and opportunities to improve and provides a sense of accomplishment that is motivational.

So, how do we effectively reflect upon our own thoughts and feelings? Here are three ways I find most useful.

- **Write.** Paul J. Meyer, an early self-improvement icon, was famous for saying, "Writing crystallizes thought." Perhaps the reason writing is so potent is that we write it as if we are speaking or thinking, yet we reflect on what we ourselves just said as if a third party was doing so. Sometimes we see the absurdity of our thoughts; other times we see the profundity of them. Either way, the insight is tremendous. Years ago, I was fortunate to attend a workshop offered by Natalie Goldberg. She taught a writing technique I use personally and offer to willing clients. You begin with a simple question or topic, such as "How I feel about . . ." Then you write, pen in hand (no typing, according to Goldberg) for ten minutes, without lifting your pen from the paper. She likes to say (I'm paraphrasing), "If your mind says, 'I am writing garbage,' then write 'I am writing garbage.'" This stream-of-consciousness method reveals much that's just below the surface, especially with some practice.

- **Engage a coach.** One of the roles a good coach serves is "thinking partner." With a coach or similar unbiased guide to ask relevant questions, listen objectively, and reflect back on what was expressed, the leader gains insight—even though, you might say, the insight was already there. You might not have the luxury of a formal coach. Mentors abound. While some of these relationships are more formal, others are offerings in which leaders can be themselves, vent, practice for tough conversations, and get good advice. If you have one of these offers, treasure it. If you can help by being a listener, volunteer.

- **Observe your thoughts and feelings.** If I say, "meditate," those of you who, like me, have tried many forms of meditation, found benefit, and failed more than succeeded, might nod and move on. Meditation as a formal practice or as a silent walk in the woods can play an important part in the leadership development cycle, and reflection can be as simple as making an objective observation of your own thoughts or feelings as you are having them. It can be a way of dis-identifying from a thought in order to assess (and discharge) its power over you. "Hmmm, did she really mean to embarrass me when she made that statement in the meeting today, or did I make that up?" Or it can be a way of clarifying a feeling and its cause. "I feel uneasy and lose my composure when Thomas enters the room. Perhaps it's time to resolve the issue we have."

Reflection requires a silencing of the noise and the demanding pull of daily life. It cannot be accomplished without a pause.

Acknowledgment

> *Acknowledgment: acceptance of the truth*
> *or existence of something.*[46]

Acknowledgment, at its most fundamental level, is honesty. We cannot act upon that which we do not accept, that which we have not acknowledged.

This practice is essential to developing the three inner qualities of compassion, courage, and humility. If we cannot acknowledge our growing edge, there is no content on which to reflect, no substance to develop. We stay stuck in our egoic rationalizations, despite messages that provide that "knock on the door" I mentioned earlier. If we cannot acknowledge our accomplishments, we appear (to ourselves) to be stuck in past patterns when, in fact, we are not, and as a result we may soon return to old behaviors. It's a bit like the person who loses significant weight yet still sees their image in the mirror as obese.

Like reflection, acknowledgment carries with it a challenge. With reflection, the danger is our mind's overidentification with whatever we are reflecting upon, reducing a powerful practice of objectivity to rumination. For acknowledgment to be an effective practice, we must be able to see ourselves clearly. And unfortunately, the way most of us see ourselves is distorted. Acknowledgment is the active cousin of self-awareness. We cannot *acknowledge* that which we do not let penetrate our consciousness, our *awareness.* In my experience, self-aware leaders can identify and acknowledge the emotions, thoughts, and behaviors that are or are not aligned with their stated values, and so on. And while self-awareness is a popular development focus and a critical leadership trait, attempts to build it and measure it are often fundamentally flawed.

Research conducted by organizational psychologist Tasha Eurich, PhD, validates this concern I have. She says true self-awareness is much rarer than we think, because power and experience cause many leaders to overestimate their skills and abilities and instill false confidence. She also says self-reflection is often done incorrectly, inviting the unwanted negative thoughts I have named here as rumination.

Four years ago, my team of researchers and I embarked on a large-scale scientific study of self-awareness. In 10 separate investigations with nearly 5,000 participants, we examined what self-awareness really is, why we need it, and how we can increase it. . . . Our research revealed many surprising roadblocks, myths, and truths about what self-awareness is and what it takes to improve it. We've found that even though most people believe they are self-aware, self-awareness is a truly rare quality: We estimate that only 10%–15% of the people we studied actually fit the criteria.[47]

According to her research, leaders who have both *internal awareness* (awareness of values and aspirations as well as thoughts, feelings, and impact on others) and *external awareness* (awareness of how others perceive you according to these same factors), the 10 to 15 percent category, "know who they are, what they want to accomplish and seek out and value others' opinions."

Acknowledgment requires honest self-assessment, which is hard yet possible, especially if one is committed to compassion (including self-compassion), courage, and humility. Let me be clear that honest self-assessment includes acknowledgment of strengths and accomplishments as well as areas in which to grow. And acknowledgment requires examining feedback from others. In my work, I gather and deliver a lot of feedback. Sometimes it's well-received, sometimes not. At a minimum, feedback requires consideration. It may not be fully accurate, or it may not match your intent, yet it always contains a message—should you be willing to acknowledge it.

Avoid, Endure . . . or Transform

In chapter three, I referenced a triad of choices one has when faced with adversity, and an opportunity to draw upon courage. This set of choices—to avoid, endure, or transform—applies to many opportunities, especially leadership development. I don't know many people whose lives are easy today, and I don't pretend to know what it's like to walk in another's shoes. A long time ago, I made a commitment to a life of personal growth and development when I chose my profession. When I find myself facing a turning point, exploring an opportunity, or teetering on the edge of a precipice, the only ultimate choice I can make from a place of integrity is to transform. The transformation might be subtle and unknown to others, or it might be significant. The reward is found in the journey. I wish that for all. We need leaders now.

Time to Reflect

1. What did you agree with strongly, and/or disagree with strongly?
2. What evoked an emotional response, and

possibly even suggested an area of personal vulnerability?

3. What one thing calls you to act, from a development perspective?

NOTES

1. James Doty, "Power of Compassion & Importance of the Work of CCARE," http://ccare.stanford.edu/videos/power-of-compassion-importance-of-the-work-of-ccare/.

2. Dr. Kristin Neff, "The Three Elements of Self-Compassion," https://self-compassion.org/the-three-elements-of-self-compassion-2/#3elements.

3. David Whyte, *Crossing the Unknown Sea: Work as a Pilgrimage of Identity* (New York: Riverhead Books, 2002), 34.

4. Sylvia Ann Hewlett, Lauren Leader-Chivée, Laura Sherbin, and Joanne Gordon with Fabiola Dieudonné, *Executive Presence*, Center for Talent Innovation.

5. Robert Greenleaf, "What Is Servant Leadership," https://www.greenleaf.org/what-is-servant-leadership/.

6. Parker Palmer, *Let Your Life Speak: Listening for the Voice of Vocation* (San Francisco: Jossey-Bass, 2000).

7. Richard Rohr, *Falling Upward: A Spirituality for the Two Halves of Life* (San Francisco: Jossey-Bass, 2011), 66.

8. Randy Hain, *Upon Reflection: Helpful Insights and Timeless Lessons for the Busy Professional* (Atlanta, GA: Serviam Press, 2022), 1.

9. "Prevent Quiet Quitting and Burnout: How to Build a Culture of Communication That Works," https://www.everythingdisc.com/insights-to-action/prevent-quiet-quitting-and-burnout-how-to-build-a-culture-of-communication-that-works.aspx.

10. "Prevent Quiet Quitting and Burnout: How to Build a Culture of Communication That Works," https://www.everythingdisc.com/insights-to-action/prevent-quiet-quitting-and-burnout-how-to-build-a-culture-of-communication-that-works.aspx.

11. Catherine Anne Lombard, "Empathy Training Shoes Part 1," https://loveandwill.com/2015/07/04/empathy-training-shoes/.

12. https://www.empathymuseum.com/a-mile-in-my-shoes/.

13. William A. Gentry, Todd J. Weber, and Golnaz Sadri, Empathy in the Workplace: A Tool for Effective Leadership, Center for Creative Leadership, 2016, https://cclinnovation. org/wp-content/uploads/2020/03/empathyintheworkplace. pdf?webSyncID=3c94ce35-baa7-a5e0-d317-8d488291ab87&se ssionGUID=598deaa8-250a-4263-60a0-9c0e9277abad.

14. Travis Bradberry and Jean Greaves, *Emotional Intelligence 2.0* (San Diego, CA: TalentSmart, 2009), 24, 38.

15. Rohr, *Falling Upward*, 128.

16. Neff, "The Three Elements of Self-Compassion."

17. David Whyte, excerpted from "The Edge You Carry with You," *Still Possible* (Langley, WA: Many Rivers Press, 2022).

18. Tara Brach, "The RAIN of Self-Compassion," https://www. tarabrach.com/selfcompassion1/.

19. Kristin Neff, PhD, *Self-Compassion: The Proven Power of Being Kind to Yourself* (New York: William Morrow, 2011), 70.

20. Nick Petrie, *Pressure Is Not Stress: 4 Steps to Be Resilient in Disruptive Times*, https://14226776-c20f-46a2-bcd6-85cefe57153f.filesusr.com/ugd/cefe74_ e9e584d886ec45dca3873d5c0d4a67ac.pdf, 13.

21. James M. Kouzes and Barry K. Posner, *Finding the Courage to Lead* (San Francisco, CA: Jossey-Bass, 2013).

22. Kouzes and Posner, *Finding the Courage to Lead*.

23. Brené Brown, *The Gifts of Imperfection* (Center City, MN: Hazelden Publishing, 2010, 2020), 20.

24. James R. Detert, "What Courageous Leaders Do Differently," Harvard Business Review, January 7, 2022, https:// hbr.org/2022/01/what-courageous-leaders-do-differently.

25. Dnika J. Travis, PhD, Emily Shaffer, PhD, and Jennifer Thorpe-Moscon, Phd, *Getting Real about Inclusive Leadership: Why Change Starts with You*, catalyst.org, https://www. catalyst.org/wp-content/uploads/2020/03/Getting-Real-About-Inclusive-Leadership-Report-2020update.pdf.

26. David Whyte, *Consolations: The Solace, Nourishment*

and Underlying Meaning of Everyday Words, Revised Edition (Langley, WA: Many Rivers Press, 2021), 49–50.

27. Dinesh C. Paliwal, "Why Inclusivity Requires the Courage to Be Uncomfortable," HuffPost, April 29, 2019, https://www.huffpost.com/entry/inclusivity-courage-to-uncomfortable_b_5b284afae4b05d6c16c657dc.

28. Paliwal, "Why Inclusivity Requires the Courage to Be Uncomfortable."

29. Colette Lafia, "The Gift of Humility," Grateful Living, https://grateful.org/resource/the-gift-of-humility/.

30. PsycInfo Database Record © 2020 APA, all rights reserved,

https://psycnet.apa.org/record/2014-42747-008.

31. Adam Grant, *Think Again: The Power of Knowing What You Don't Know* (New York: Viking, 2021), 47.

32. Grant, *Think Again*, 46.

33.*Think Again*, 46.

34. Tim Burkett, "The Wisdom of Humility," HuffPost, June 13, 2016, https://www.huffpost.com/entry/the-wisdom-of-humility_b_10437020.

35. Shunryu Suzuki, *Zen Mind, Beginner's Mind*, 50th Anniversary Edition (Boulder, CO: Shambhala Publications, 2020).

36. Dan Cable, "How Humble Leadership Really Works," April 23, 2018, *Harvard Business Review*, https://hbr.org/2018/04/how-humble-leadership-really-works.

37. Shelby Scarbrough, "After You: Humility As A Core Leadership Skill," February 24, 2022, *Forbes*, https://www.forbes.com/sites/forbesbooksauthors/2022/02/04/after-you-humility-as-a-core-leadership-skill/?sh=76a2b4d877f5.

38. *Think Again*, 48, 106.

39. Kevin Kruse, "Servant Leadership Is Not What You Think: Ken Blanchard Explains," *Forbes*, April 9, 2018, https://www.forbes.com/sites/kevinkruse/2018/04/09/servant-leadership-is-not-what-you-think-ken-blanchard-explains/?sh=3f7ac7806a5f.

40. *Think Again*, 137.

41. David Whyte, excerpted from the poem "Start Close In" in *Essentials* (Langley, WA: Many Rivers Press, 2022), 13.

42. Carl Jung, *Psychology and Religion* (New Haven, CT: Yale University Press, 1938), 131.

43. Rohr, *Falling Upward*, 128.

44. Dr. Geil Browning, "Make Time for Personal Reflection," Emergenetics International, https://emergenetics.com/blog/make-time-for-personal-reflection/.

45. Michelle Hlubinka, "Reflection," The Clubhouse Learning Approach, https://web.media.mit.edu/~mres/clubhouse/handouts/reflection-v6.pdf.

46. *Oxford English Dictionary*.

47. Tasha Eurich, "What Self-Awareness Really Is (and How to Cultivate It)," *Harvard Business Review*, January 4, 2018, https://hbr.org/2018/01/what-self-awareness-really-is-and-how-to-cultivate-it.

Made in the USA
Columbia, SC
15 July 2023

20479954R00055